FEEDING THE WORLD

Corn

Feeding the World

CORN

DAIRY PRODUCTS

EGGS

FARMED FISH

MEAT

RICE

SOYBEANS

WHEAT

FEEDING THE WORLD
Corn

KIM ETINGOFF

MASON CREST

Mason Crest
450 Parkway Drive, Suite D
Broomall, PA 19008
www.masoncrest.com

Printed and bound in the United States of America.

First printing
9 8 7 6 5 4 3 2 1

Series ISBN: 978-1-4222-2741-1
ISBN: 978-1-4222-2742-8
ebook ISBN: 978-1-4222-9074-3

The Library of Congress has cataloged the

hardcopy format(s) as follows:

Library of Congress Cataloging-in-Publication Data

Etingoff, Kim.
  Corn / Kim Etingoff.
      p. cm. — (Feeding the world)
  ISBN 978-1-4222-2742-8 (hardcover) — ISBN 978-1-4222-2741-1 (series) — ISBN 978-1-4222-9074-3 (ebook)
  1. Corn—Juvenile literature. 2. Food supply—Juvenile literature. I. Title. II. Series: Feeding the world.
  SB191.M2E85 2014
  635'.67—dc23
                                    2013004736

Publisher's notes:
The websites mentioned in this book were active at the time of publication. The publisher is not responsible for websites that have changed their addresses or discontinued operation since the date of publication. The publisher will review and update the website addresses each time the book is reprinted.

CONTENTS

CHAPTER ONE

Where Does Corn Come From?

You open your refrigerator and look inside. What do you see? Maybe a jug of milk. Jars with different foods inside. Some leftovers from last night's dinner. Fruits and vegetables.

Have you ever thought about where all that food comes from? It doesn't just show up in the refrigerator by magic!

Sure, your family probably bought it at the grocery store. But what about before that? Grocery stores don't grow vegetables. They don't raise chickens for meat. They don't make their own yogurt and put it into cups.

Before the store, the food you eat had to come from wherever it was made, grown, or raised. Food comes from many different places around the world.

If you have a garden, some of the veggies in your refrigerator might have grown right in your backyard. Or they could have been grown on a big farm halfway across the world. The milk on the top shelf might have come from the other side of the country. A farmer in your town may have grown the apples you eat.

THE BASICS

In the end, almost all of the food you eat comes from the earth. It's easy to imagine how a carrot gets from the ground to your stomach. It's harder to figure out just how cookies from the store start out.

Carrots are pretty simple. A farmer grows carrots and then sends them to a warehouse. The warehouse keeps the carrots until sending them to grocery stores. Then, people like you buy them and bring them home.

Cookies are different. They don't grow in the ground or come from a farm. Think about the **ingredients** in a cookie. There's flour made from ground-up wheat. Cookies are made with sugar. They might also have baking powder, eggs, and chocolate chips.

Farmers grow many of the ingredients that go into cookies. They grow wheat and sugar. Other farmers raise the chickens that lay the eggs and the cows that give the milk. Farmers also raise cacao beans, which become chocolate. Factories make the baking powder from natural **chemicals**. All those ingredients end up in factories where workers make the cookies. The cookies are sent from the factory to the grocery store. Then, someone in your family buys a package at the store and brings the cookies home to eat.

GROW YOUR OWN

If you are really curious about where food comes from, grow some yourself! It's pretty easy to grow a garden full of veggies. Just get a bunch of seeds and plant them in dirt. Make sure your seeds get plenty of sun and water and then see what happens. Choose vegetables you know you already like. Or choose some you haven't tried before. Watch as your seeds grow into tomatoes, beans, lettuce, and more.

The food we buy at the grocery store comes from many different places around the world. All the food that we eat has a long story about how it got from a farm to your plate.

Where Does Corn Come From? 9

THE PEOPLE WHO MAKE FOOD

Whether it's a carrot or a cookie, there are many people who work to make all the food you eat.

Farmers grow fruits and vegetables and raise animals. Truck drivers, pilots, or ship captains move food around from one place to another. Factory workers and machines put ingredients together and package food. Grocery store workers sell food. People buy it. And you eat it!

Without all those people, the way we get food would be very different. Very few people grow and make everything they eat. We all depend on other people to get our food.

EVEN MORE PEOPLE

There are actually a lot more people who help you get food. People work hard to figure out the best way to sell food. Some work on commercials to get you to want to buy the food they make. Construction workers build the factories where food is made and grocery stores where it's sold. Chefs cook food in restaurants. In the end, thousands and thousands of workers are all part of getting food to people around the world.

TAKING A LOOK AT CORN

People eat a lot of corn today. We eat fresh corn on the cob. We eat popcorn. We eat corn from a can. We also eat corn that's hidden in other food.

Most of the animals we eat as meat eat lots of corn. In a way, we eat corn whenever we eat beef, pork, chicken, and other meat. Corn is a cheap way for farmers to feed animals they raise. Most of the corn that farmers grow around the world ends up in the stomachs of cows, chicken, pigs, and other animals. Then it makes its way to you when you eat meat.

You also eat corn in lots of **processed** foods. Processed foods are things like crackers, cookies, and chips. Ingredients go to a factory, where people make them into processed food. Processed foods don't grow outside like fruits, vegetables, grains, or meats, but they are made from those things.

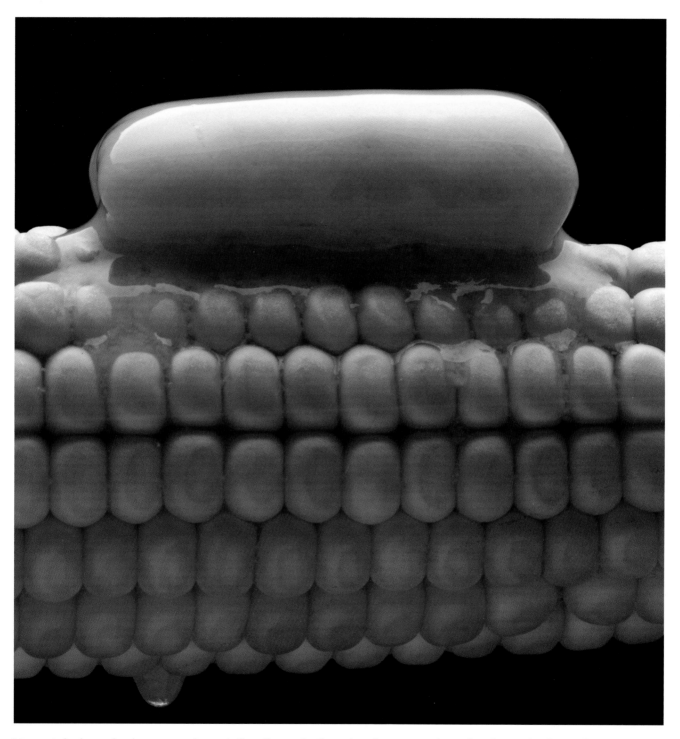

You might have had corn on the cob for dinner before, but have you thought about the farm that corn comes from? Even the butter you put on your corn started as milk on a farm!

Where Does Corn Come From? 11

Did you know that even cheeseburgers have corn in them? The animals we eat as meat (cows, pigs, chickens, and more) eat corn. When we eat a burger (meat from a cow), we're eating the corn that the cow ate.

Most processed foods have at least one ingredient that's made from corn. Most of the corn we eat in processed food is called high fructose corn syrup. It's a type of really sweet sugar that's made from corn. High fructose corn syrup is in lots and lots of processed foods. It's in soda, ketchup, jelly, canned soup, and more. Even though we might not always know it, we eat a lot of corn.

12   Corn

The corn we eat starts with the farmers who plant the seeds. They take care of the corn as it grows, and then **harvest** it. The farmers send it to grocery stores. Or they send it to factories that make it into high fructose corn syrup or feed for animals. Then it makes its way to you in one way or another. Every bit of corn you eat has its own story!

NOT JUST FOR FOOD

You can find corn in things that aren't food too. Cleaning detergent, chewing gum, plastic, tires, makeup, and sandpaper all have things made from corn in them. That doesn't mean that we can eat these things! But it does mean that corn is a very useful plant for a lot of different people.

Some corn gets turned into fuel for our cars. Fuel made from corn is called ethanol. The country of Brazil uses a lot of ethanol. If your family has a car, check the pump next time your parents get gas. There might be a sign saying the gas you're putting in your car has ethanol.

CHAPTER TWO

The History of Corn

Today, we eat a lot of corn. In the past, people ate lots of corn too. People have been eating corn for a long time. We're keeping a food **tradition** alive!

IN THE BEGINNING

Corn first started growing in Central America and Mexico. But corn didn't always look like the corn we know today. It looked completely different.

Thousands of years ago, corn didn't have big **ears**. It had tiny seeds. It looked more like grass. That's because corn is a kind of grass.

Native people in Central America found that they could eat the seeds of the grass plant. It was really hard to harvest the seeds, though. They were tiny!

The plant also grew in the wild. People didn't always know where to look for it.

So, people decided to create a new plant. They took the grass plants that had the biggest seeds and planted those. Once those plants grew up, they planted the biggest seeds again. Over time, the plant started to look very different. The seeds in each new set of plants got bigger and bigger. After some time, the plants looked like the corn that we know today.

People also learned how to grow corn themselves. They figured out how to plant it in fields. Now people didn't have to go out and find plants to pick the seeds. They could grow corn where they wanted to, so it was easier to find.

LEGENDS

Many Native American groups had their own stories about where corn came from. Here's a legend told by a Sauk leader in 1833. The Sauk are a group of natives from northern North America.

I will relate the manner in which corn first came. According to tradition handed down to our people, a beautiful woman was seen to descend from the clouds, and alight upon the earth, by two of our ancestors who had killed a deer, and were sitting by a fire roasting a part of it to eat. They were astonished at seeing her, and concluded that she was hungry and had smelt the meat. They immediately went to her, taking with them a piece of the roasted venison. They presented it to her, she ate it, telling them to return to the spot where she was sitting at the end of one year, and they would find a reward for their kindness and generosity. She then ascended to the clouds and disappeared. The men returned to their village, and explained to the tribe what they had seen, done and heard, but were laughed at by their people. When the period had arrived for them to visit this consecrated ground, where they were to find a reward for their attention to the beautiful woman of the clouds, they went with a large party, and found where her right hand had rested on the ground corn growing, where the left hand had rested beans, and immediately where she had been seated, tobacco. (www.native-languages.org/saukstory.htm)

16   Corn

Corn grows in huge fields, with all the corn plants lined up in rows. Some farmers have thousands of corn plants growing all in one field.

CORN BECOMES POPULAR

For a while, corn only grew in one small area in Central America. Then it started spreading to more places. People from Central America taught others how to grow corn.

Cornbread is just one of the many foods people make from corn. Cornbread is baked in a pan and usually has a sweet taste. Some people spread butter or honey on their cornbread.

People were excited about corn. It was easy to grow. It tasted good. They could make a lot of different food from corn. Different native groups began to farm corn in South America. It spread to North America too.

People were farming corn all the way from the bottom of South America to the middle of North America. It turned out that corn was easy to grow in lots of different types of dirt. It could also grow in hotter places and colder places.

18   **Corn**

People have been making corn tortillas for hundreds of years. Some corn tortillas are different colors, depending on the color of the corn they're made from. You can even get blue tortillas made from blue corn!

Corn was a really important food. It became a staple crop. That means people ate corn just about every day, with every meal. Most corn was dried and pounded into flour. After that, people made it into breads, fried cakes, tortillas, and more.

So far, only people in the Americas knew about corn. The rest of the world hadn't heard about it.

Then, Europeans started coming to the Americas in the 1500s. They were explorers from Spain, Portugal, England, and other parts of Europe. The Europeans saw that everyone was eating corn. They tried it too.

Today people eat corn all over the world in many different ways. There is canned corn, popcorn, corn on the cob, and more. Corn is also in a lot of other foods, from soda to meat.

20 **Corn**

The Europeans thought that corn was a good food. When they went back to Europe, they took corn with them. Europeans called corn "maize."

Pretty soon, people all over Europe were eating corn, just like the people in the Americas. From there, corn kept spreading around the world.

CORN TODAY

Now, corn is a food that everyone enjoys all over the world. Corn is still an important food in Central America. Remember, that's where it started growing a long time ago.

People in almost every part of the world eat corn. Just about everyone knows what corn is!

CORNY NAMES

Different groups of people call corn different things. People in Canada and the United States use the word corn. Other English speakers say maize. In South Africa, people call it mealie.

CHAPTER THREE

Who Grows the Corn We Eat?

Corn doesn't grow only in the Americas anymore. Lots of farmers in countries around the world grow corn.

COUNTRIES CORN COMES FROM

The United States grows the most corn in the world. In fact, it grows about 40 percent of the world's corn. That means that if you had 100 bags of corn, 40 of them would have come from the United States.

The middle of the United States grows the most corn. The land is flat, and the dirt (also called soil) is good for growing things. There are fields and fields of corn in this part of the United States. The fields can be huge.

Chinese farmers work hard to farm corn for hungry people all over the world. China is one of the biggest corn-farming countries in the world. Only the United States farms more corn than China.

 **24** **Corn**

The United States ends up growing so much corn that Americans can't even use it all. Instead, some of the corn is sent to other countries. Some countries don't grow much corn. But they want corn. So they buy it from countries that have too much, like the United States.

People in the United States also eat the most corn in the world. On average, each American eats 160 pounds of corn in a year. That's as much as a person weighs!

China grows the second-largest amount of corn. Corn has grown in China since the 1550s. Corn grows all over the country. Many farmers grow corn in the northeastern and the southern parts of China.

A lot of people eat corn in China, too. People in China eat the second-largest amount of corn in the world, after the United States.

There are lots of other countries that grow corn too. In Central America, Mexico grows a lot of corn, just like in the past. In South America, farmers in Brazil and Argentina grow lots of corn. So do farmers in France, India, Italy, Romania, and South Africa. Corn is grown all around the world!

CORN FARMERS

Corn farmers have a big job. They have to grow a lot of corn. So who are these people?

They could be anyone! They could live in China, or Mexico, or the United States. Lots of corn farmers grew up in families that raised corn. They're doing the same thing that their parents and grandparents did.

Corn farmers usually live in the countryside. Some live on their farms. It's hard to farm a lot of corn if you live in a busy city. Farmers need lots of room for big fields of corn.

During some years, farmers make a lot of money selling their corn. In other years, things can be harder. A **drought** might kill fields of corn. Some years, the price of corn might be really low. That makes it hard for corn farmers to make enough money. If a farmer sells her corn for more than another farmer does, people might not buy the first farmer's corn because it costs too much.

Corn farmers have to be willing to take chances. Farming isn't always easy. Things can change from year to year for many farmers.

CHAPTER FOUR

How Is Corn Grown?

It takes a little while for corn to grow from a seed into a nice, big **cob**. Corn grows just like other plants. Farmers have to be patient and care for the growing plant. Then, when it's done growing, they can harvest the corn they've been waiting for.

SEED TO STALK

The first step to growing a plant is, of course, to plant the seed! With corn, the seeds are the **kernels**. Think about popcorn. Each piece of popcorn is a kernel, and each kernel is a seed. When you eat corn on the cob, each yellow or white bit of corn is a seed. Each one could grow into a new corn plant if you planted it.

Farmers usually plant a lot of corn at one time. They don't grow just ten corn plants. They grow hundreds or thousands. They have to plant a lot of seeds to get enough corn to make money.

They use a machine to help them plant the seeds. It would take weeks to plant 10,000 seeds by hand. Machines make the work much easier.

After a week or so, the seeds start to slowly turn into a corn plant. Now the corn is a **seedling**. Seedlings need a few things to grow well: water, dirt, sun, and the right temperature. It can't be too cold or too warm, or the seedlings won't live long. Farmers have to think carefully about when to plant their corn.

At first, corn just looks like grass. It has a few small, flat, green leaves. As it grows bigger, it starts to look different. It gets a tall, thick **stalk**. The stalk has many big, flat leaves too.

Under the ground, the roots are growing. Roots help the plant hold on to the dirt. They also suck up food and water from the soil.

PLANT YOUR OWN CORN

If you have a little extra space, ask your parents if you can plant your own corn! Make sure you're starting after the last frost in your area. First, get some seeds. You'll want to plant some kind of sweet corn, which you can eat fresh. You might need to add fertilizer or compost to the soil to make sure it's healthy. Plant the corn seeds in a square. Plant each seed about two inches deep and six inches apart.

Pretty soon, seedlings will pop up. When they're a few inches high, pull out some of the seedlings. Pulling them out leaves room for the rest of the corn to grow big. Leave big, healthy seedlings a foot apart. Water your plants if the soil looks dry or the corn starts to look faded or droopy. Pull weeds that grow up around your plants.

When the ears look big, take a look at the kernels. Poke them with your fingernail. If a white liquid comes out, they're ready to harvest, and super sweet. Pick the ears and eat them right away!

28   **Corn**

STALK TO HARVEST

After a couple of months of growing, the corn plant starts to grow what looks like hair. The hair shows up about halfway up the stalk. We call the hair corn silk. Every corn silk is attached to one kernel of corn.

Corn silk looks a bit like hair coming from the top of an ear of corn. At first, the silks are green but they soon become yellow or red.

All corn begins with planting some seeds. If you have corn seeds, you can even plant your own corn. On big farms, with many corn plants, farmers use machines to help plant the seeds.

At the top of the plant, long things called tassels also grow. The tassels make **pollen**. The goal is for the pollen from the tassels to get to the corn silks. Wind carries the pollen from corn plant to corn plant.

Once the pollen gets to the silks, the kernels start to grow bigger. They are growing into seeds. All together, the kernels make up the ear of corn.

HARVESTING

The farmer has to keep a close eye on the ears of corn. If she harvests the corn too soon, it won't be as big as it could be. If she harvests the corn too late, it gets too tough and dried out.

Farmers pick corn that is juicy for eating. But other farmers might want to let it dry on the stalk. Popcorn has to be drier than fresh corn ready for eating. Most of the corn that animals eat has to

30   Corn

be picked while it's dry. So does the corn that's used to make other food. The farmer will wait until the whole corn plant is brown and dead before harvesting it.

Once it's time, the farmer picks the corn. For fresh corn, the farmer could pick the cobs by hand. On larger farms, there are thousands of rows of corn to harvest. It would take a very long time to harvest them all by hand.

Instead, farmers use machines called combine harvesters. They are big machines on wheels that go down the rows of plants. Combine harvesters pull all the corn kernels from the cob. They leave the cob and the leaves in the field.

After harvesting, the corn is ready to move on to the next steps in it's trip from the farm to your plate.

Farmers use combine harvesters like this one to get the corn from the fields. On farms with thousands of corn plants, there are too many plants that need harvesting to have people do the work by themselves.

How Is Corn Grown?

Watering fields of corn can take a lot of water. Using that much water to keep corn healthy costs farmers a lot of money.

 **32** **Corn**

HELPING PLANTS GROW

Farmers don't just sit back and watch while their corn crops grow. They have to help their corn grow sometimes.

Corn grows best in dirt with a lot of **nutrients**. You need to eat the right food to be healthy. So do corn plants!

Farmers often add nutrients to the dirt to help corn grow. Some farmers add fertilizer (animal poop) with nutrients in it. Other farmers add compost, which is recycled, dead plants. Compost also has a lot of nutrients in it.

While the corn is growing, farmers have to water it sometimes too. It doesn't always rain enough for corn to grow. If it's too dry, farmers might have to water their crops.

Watering huge fields can cost a lot of money. Farmers keep their fingers crossed that it rains enough. But not too much, or their fields will flood. Farming can be risky!

ORGANIC FARMING

Most farmers who grow food to sell use things like chemical fertilizers and pesticides. But not all farmers want to use those things. Chemicals can get into the water and poison animals and other creatures (including humans). Pesticides kill all bugs, even though some bugs are good for the farm, like bees and spiders. Farmers who don't want to use chemicals choose to grow food organically. They don't use chemical pesticides and fertilizers that could hurt the environment. Organic farmers work with nature to grow food. They use compost and natural pesticides like clay or copper.

Organic farms are found all over the world. They are often smaller than non-organic farms, but that isn't always true. Organic farming is becoming more popular. There are organic vegetables, fruits, grains, meat, and more. Maybe you've even eaten some organic food from the grocery store or the farmers' market. Organic food has a label that says it's organic. Take a look the next time you're at the store.

Before corn grows into a tall stalk, it starts as a small seedling like these. Seedlings are just a few inches tall. When corn is fully-grown, its stalk is usually a few feet tall.

34 Corn

Weeds are always a problem too. Weeds are plants that are growing where you don't want them. To get rid of weeds, farmers can pull them out by hand. They can also use chemicals to kill them. They could use tractors to pull them up. Or they could put something on the dirt to keep weeds from getting sun and growing big. Farmers might use bark chips, cut grass, hay, or other things to keep weeds from growing.

Farmers also have to worry about bugs and other pests. We're not the only ones that want to eat corn. So do lots of bugs, deer, and other creatures.

Farmers have figured out how to protect their plants. They can spray pesticides on them. Pesticides are chemicals that kill bugs. They can put sheets over the plants to hide them from bugs. They can also put up fences to keep out bigger animals, like deer.

CHAPTER FIVE

How Does Corn Get to Your Plate?

Growing the corn is only half the story. It still has to travel from the field to your plate. There are many paths corn can take. It can be a long trip!

WHAT ABOUT FRESH CORN?

Not all the corn we eat is hidden. Some of it looks like corn! You can go to the store and buy corn on the cob. You can also buy frozen or canned corn.

Fresh corn has the shortest number of steps from the farm to you. The farmer picks it. Then he sends it to a warehouse. Finally, the warehouse ships it to a grocery store.

The farmer might also sell his own corn at a local farmers' market. Farmers set up tables to sell what they grow. Customers buy their food right from the farmer!

On farms that can't afford machines to help them dry their corn, farmers let corn dry in the sun by hanging it up like this.

38 **Corn**

Frozen and canned corn have a couple more steps. First, farmers harvest corn. Then they send the corn to a factory. There, the corn is frozen and put in packages or cans. After that, the factory sends it to the warehouse where it sits, waiting to go to the store. Finally, it's on to the grocery store where someone buys it.

DRYING

Most of the corn farmers grow isn't sold as fresh corn. It turns into animal food. Or it becomes cereal or high fructose corn syrup, a kind of sugar used in many foods. After that, corn has a different journey.

After a farmer harvests all her corn, she has to let it dry. If she sends it somewhere while it's still wet, the corn won't last.

Farmers can get special dryers for their corn. Once they put their fresh corn in the dryer, it takes a few hours to dry. It comes out looking shriveled up and hard.

STORING

When farmers harvest their corn all at the same time during the season, there's a lot of corn around. People don't want to eat corn all at once!

The best thing for farmers to do is keep it for a while. Some farmers keep their corn on their farm. They have huge containers for all the corn they grow and dry. It can last for a long time.

Other farmers send their corn to big buildings made to store corn. Lots of farmers store their corn in the same place. When farmers need more corn, they can take it out of storage.

MILLS

The corn isn't much use just sitting around. It still has a ways to go before it becomes food.

Some corn goes to a mill. Mills grind up the corn until it becomes flour or corn meal. Imagine pounding up some dried corn until it looks like powder.

Mills also separate corn kernels into their different parts. Each kernel has an outside, called a hull. It also has two other parts inside called a germ and starch.

Next, mills send each part to different places. The germ and hulls are sent to companies that sell animal feed. Cows and other animals will eat them.

Even soda has corn in it! Soda is made with high fructose corn syrup, which is made from corn in big factories.

The starchy parts are sent to food factories. They will become cereal, chips, crackers, and more. The starch will also become high fructose corn syrup.

FACTORIES

Each part of the corn goes to its own factory. Every factory does something different with its corn to make whatever food it sells.

Factories have ways of changing bits of corn into all sorts of foods. Some add chemicals and water to corn. Then they turn the corn into high fructose corn syrup.

Some factories make foods that are mostly corn. Think about tortilla chips, or corn flakes. Other factories make foods that are made with just a little bit of corn, like soda.

You wouldn't be able to spot corn after it comes out of a factory. It looks like a cracker or juice, not like corn!

Factories also put the food they make in packages. Otherwise, it would be hard to send all that food to the next step. Packages also make it easy to store food and take it home.

A lot of the corn grown around the world goes to feed animals like cows, chickens, and pigs. That's why when we eat meat from these animals, we're also eating the corn they ate!

How Does Corn Get to Your Plate? 41

From the farm to your popcorn bowl, each kernel of corn has had a long trip from the farm to get to you. Remember that next time you make popcorn before watching a movie with your family!

 **42** **Corn**

ANIMALS

Not all corn is sent to a factory. Some of it is sent to people who raise animals. Corn is mixed with other food and given to cows, pigs, chickens, and even fish.

After a while, animals get big enough that it's time to kill them. That's how they become meat, after all. They are sent to factories where they are killed and cut up into pieces of meat.

Meat might not look like corn, but it sort of is. The animal the meat came from ate a lot of corn. It turned all that corn into muscle and fat. You can say that you're eating corn when you eat meat.

WAREHOUSES

Now the meat or corn products make their way to warehouses. Grocery stores own warehouses to hold all of the food they want to sell.

In the warehouse, workers sort through all the food that comes in. All of those corn products are split up. Not every box of cereal will be going to the same place. Some will go to one part of the country. Others will end up far away from there.

When all the food is sorted, it gets loaded on to trucks for the next step.

MOVING AROUND

Every time the corn moves from place to place, someone has to do the moving. So, first the corn moved from the farm to storage. Then it moved to a factory. Next, it moved to a warehouse and on to a grocery store. Finally, it moved to your home.

Corn can move a really long way. A farmer might raise corn thousands of miles from where a customer buys it. Or even on the other side of the world.

So how does corn get from one place to another? Trucks, trains, planes, and boats! If it isn't going very far, corn might travel in a big truck. Or it might be faster to put it in a train, plane, or boat if it has to go really far.

GROCERY STORES

Finally, we're almost getting to the part where you come in! From the warehouse or the meat factory, corn products are sent to grocery stores.

Most of the corn we're following is hidden now. You have to read food labels to figure out if there's any corn in the food you're buying. You can bet that a lot of things in the grocery store have corn in them.

Stores put out all the corn products on their shelves. There's corn in the fresh fruits and vegetable part of the store. There's corn in the frozen and canned food aisles. There's corn in the meat, and the milk (because cows that are milked ate corn too). There's corn in the snack food aisle. Just about every part of the store has food made with corn.

The final step is the **customer**. People come into the store and buy all that corn. You and your family are some of those customers!

We don't always think about where our food comes from. It doesn't come from the fridge or the grocery store. People work hard to grow it in the ground. So next time you take a bite of corn, think for a minute. Think about all the steps it took for that corn to get to you. You have lots of people to thank for that one bite!

WORDS TO KNOW:

chemicals: Something created by scientists that can change something else when the two are mixed.

cob: The center part of the corn, covered in kernels.

customer: A person who buys something, including food.

drought: A time when little or no rain falls.

ears: The part of the corn where kernels grow on the cob, covered in thin leaves.

harvest: Gathering grown plants on a farm.

kernels: The small, yellow or white part of the corn that we eat.

ingredients: Different foods that are mixed together to make a new food.

nutrients: Vitamins and minerals that help plants (and people) grow strong and healthy.

pollen: Groups of tiny plant parts that help plants grow and spread. Together, many pollen grains look like dust.

processed: The way ingredients are mixed or changed in a factory to become the food we eat.

seedling: A young plant.

stalk: The thick stem of a plant.

tradition: A way of doing things that has been used for many years.

FIND OUT MORE

Online

Camp Silos
www.campsilos.org/mod3/students/index.shtml

Quiz: Where Does this Food Come From?
www.1millionacts.com.au/inspiration/kids-quiz-where-does-this-food-come-from

Where Your Food Comes From
urbanext.illinois.edu/food

In Books

Gibbons, Gail. *Corn*. New York: Holiday House, 2009.

Micucci, Charles. *The Life and Times of Corn*. New York: Houghton Mifflin, 2009.

Reilly, Kathleen M. *Food: 25 Amazing Projects*. White River Junction, Ver: Nomad Press, 2010.

INDEX

ABOUT THE AUTHOR

Kim Etingoff lives in Boston, Massachusetts, spending part of her time working on farms. Kim enjoys connecting people of all ages to agriculture and teaching others where their food comes from.

PICTURE CREDITS